The Choice Is Yours

An Art Activity Handbook for Young Artists

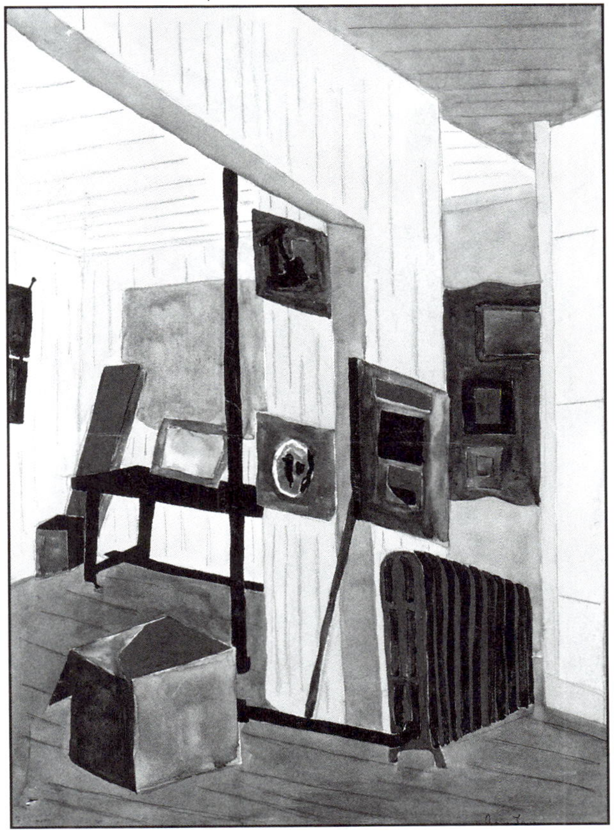

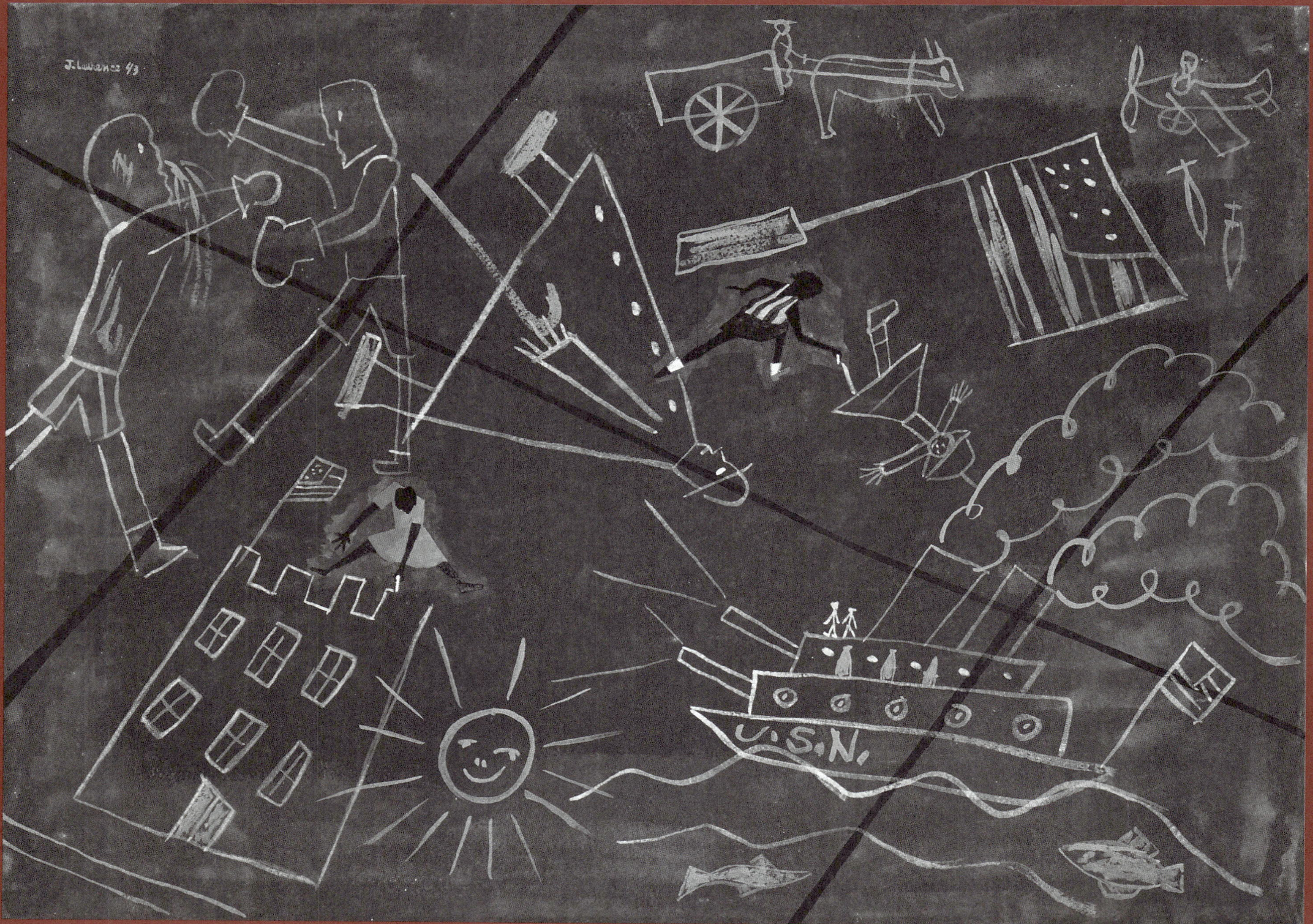
J. Lawrence 43
U.S.N.

The Choice Is Yours

An Art Activity Handbook for Young Artists

Highlighting the Art and Life of Jacob Lawrence

Suzanne **Wright**

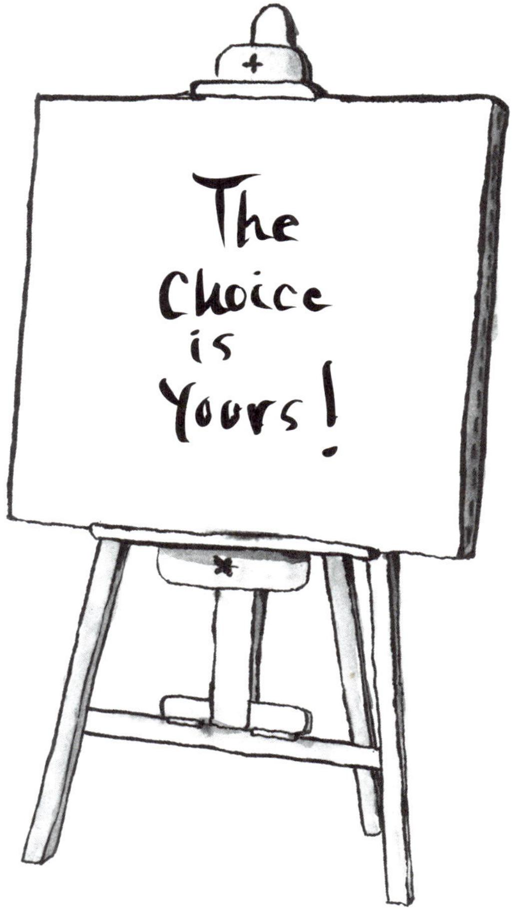

To be used with
I See You, I See Myself:
The Young Life of Jacob Lawrence
by Deba Foxley Leach

The Phillips Collection
Washington, D.C.

Contents

Contents

Introduction

This activity book has been designed for you. We hope it sparks your **imagination** and gives you the **freedom** to make **choices** in your life and through your art.

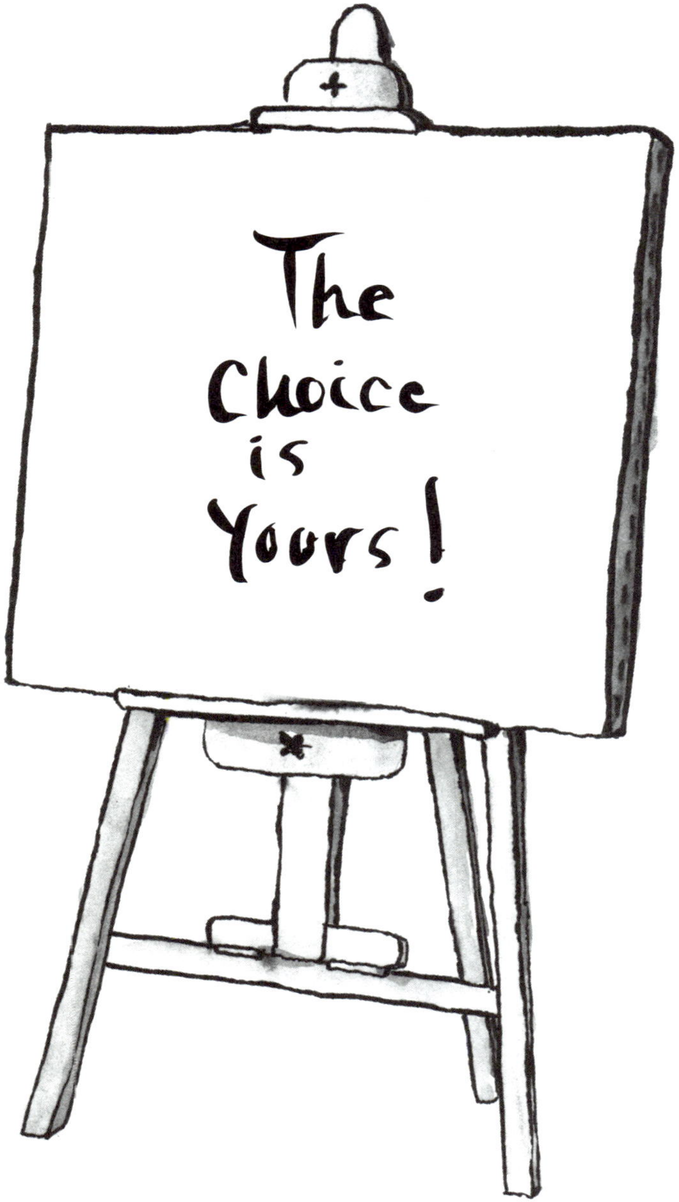

An artist may not have a lot of control over other things in his or her life, but in the picture's space the artist makes the **decisions**.

You will see the word **composition** often in this handbook. The composition of a picture is the way that you, the artist, arrange your choices in a picture.

Artist's Language

In this handbook, you will find chapter headings like this.

These introduce different elements or parts of the **artist's language**. You learn the artist's language the same way you learn Spanish, French or a sport, step by step and with a lot of practice. On these pages you will find art games about the art elements line, shape, pattern, and color to name just a few.

Art Choice

On almost every page you will find the symbol **art choice**. This is your opportunity to make choices about art through fun drawing games and activities. Remember, the choice is yours.

Jacob Lawrence was a wonderful artist. His life, art, and ideas are presented throughout this handbook. Look for pages called **The Story of Jacob Lawrence**. This artist's story is not only interesting, but could also be a springboard for thinking about your own life. (To learn more about Jacob Lawrence, read *I See You, I See Myself.*)

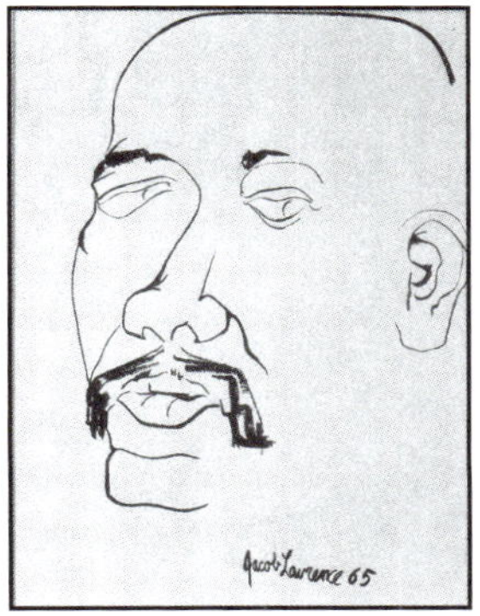

Throughout the handbook look for pages called **Sense of Self**. These pages have been specially designed with "idea starters" to help you imagine how your feelings and experiences (at home, in the neighborhood, or in your community) could spark ideas for works of art!

Idea Starter

These help spark your memory and your feelings and possibly inspire a work of art!

You will also find **experiment pages**. These are blank pages for you to write down your ideas, draw, create your own art games, or leave blank. The choice is yours.

Turn the page to begin making choices.

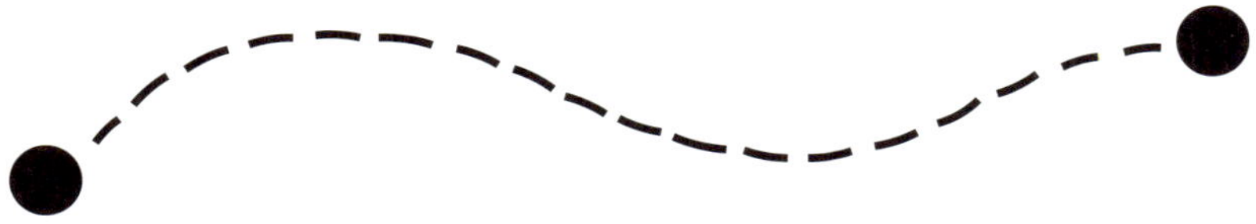

Welcome to your new language, the artist's language. When you were learning to read, the first thing you learned was the alphabet.

Line is the first thing you learn in the artist's language.

A line can be defined as a point that moves through space and time.

Artists use lines to **communicate** ideas. You can use lines to doodle, draw, paint, or write your name. You can press very hard to make a thick, bold line or press very gently to make a thin, quiet line. Artists like to use many types of lines.

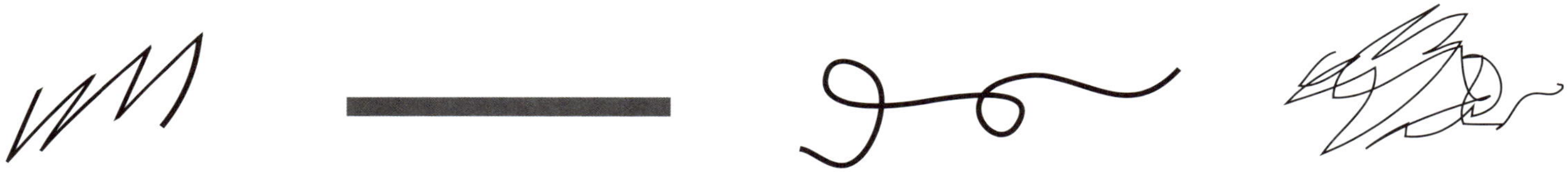

jagged straight & wide loopy thin & messy

Art Choice

Did you know that artists use lines to show their **feelings**? Different kinds of lines can express different feelings. Experiment. Draw a line or lines in each box to describe the feeling written below the box. (There are no right or wrong answers.)

happiness

sadness

excitement

anticipation

anxiety

The lines that you draw can look like they are moving. These lines have **motion**.

Diagonal lines seem to move fast.
(Think of a tree falling.)

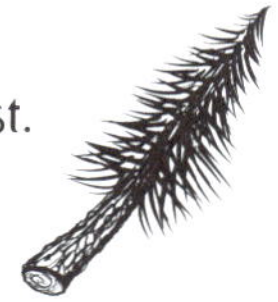

Vertical lines don't move as fast.
(Think of a tree that *could* fall.)

Horizontal lines seem to move more slowly.
(Think of a person sleeping.)

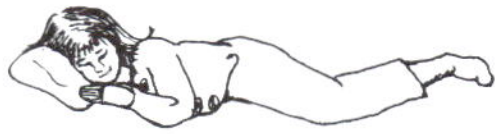

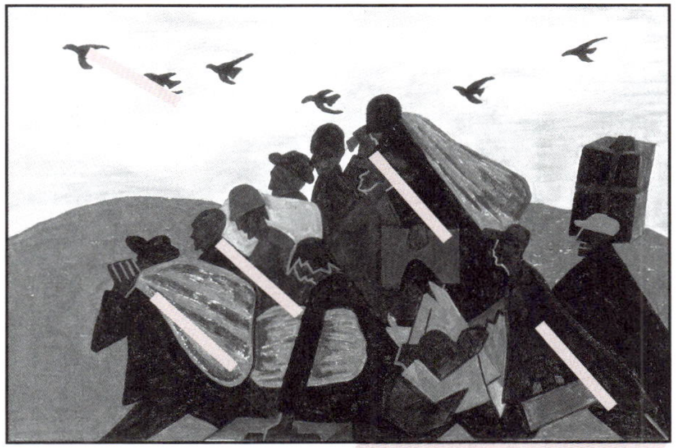

Jacob Lawrence, *The Migration Series, No. 3,* 1940–41.

Did Jacob Lawrence use horizontal, diagonal, or vertical lines to make the people look like they are moving in this painting? ____________

Do you remember doing "connect the dots" when you were little? Artists draw with lines that are *implied* by putting dots or people or things in a row. Your eyes must "connect the dots" to make the line. Notice how Jacob Lawrence drew the birds in *The Migration Series*. Draw a line to connect the birds. This is the path that Jacob Lawrence wanted your eyes to follow.

Art Choice

In these boxes draw lines that express:

- being late to catch a bus
- waiting in line
- Can you think of something else: ____________

(Try using implied lines and line direction.)

Moving

The Story of Jacob Lawrence

Jacob Lawrence's paintings are often based on his own **experiences**. Moving was one experience that Lawrence was very familiar with. As a child he moved several times. When he was a young man, Lawrence painted a group of paintings about moving called ***The Migration Series.*** In 60 paintings, Lawrence shows the move of over a million African Americans from farms in the South to cities in the North in search of a better life. Through his pictures, Lawrence wanted to show that moving could be a good thing, but it was complicated, and could have many moments of struggle, sadness, and difficulty.

Idea Starter

Artists often are looking for ideas. They write them down or sketch them in a notebook or on scraps of paper. They might keep them for a while before making a work of art from them.

By filling in the blanks below, these "idea starters" might spark your memory and your feelings about moving.

Have you ever moved? ________

List three things you liked about moving.

1. ________
2. ________
3. ________

List three things you didn't like about moving.

1. ________
2. ________
3. ________

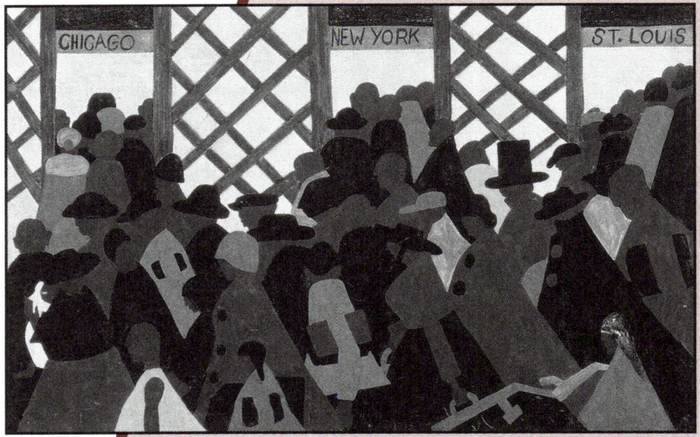

Jacob Lawrence, *The Migration Series, No. 1*, 1940–41.

Sense of *Self*

Naming Your Line

Your **signature** is a line that expresses who you are.

Art Choice

Try these signature "warm-ups." Follow the directions for each box. Don't worry about staying in the boxes. These warm-ups really get the creativity going!

Write your name with your eyes closed.

Write your name with your other hand. For example, if you're right-handed, use your left hand.

Write your name backwards, by starting with the last letter in your name.

Art Choice

Try out three different signatures in the boxes below. Which one seems to best describe who you are?

Divide Space Using Line

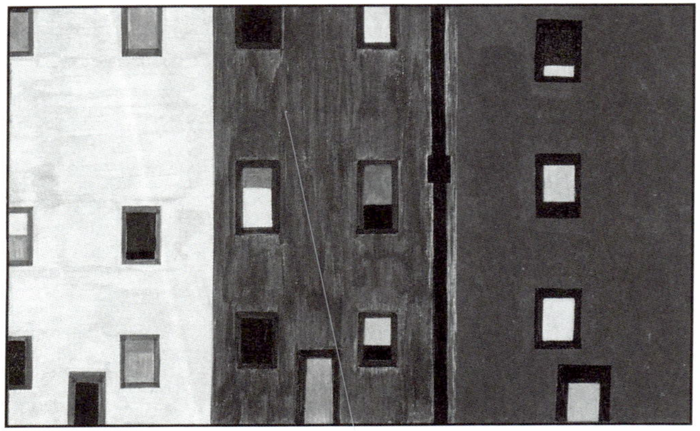

Jacob Lawrence, *The Migration Series, No. 31*, 1940–41.

Now that you've started to make choices such as your signature, let's look at one important choice that an artist makes.

One of the first choices that an artist makes in a picture is about dividing **space**. Look at Jacob Lawrence's *The Migration Series, No. 31*. This is a painting of apartment buildings in a city. Lawrence has divided the picture's space into three almost equal sections.

After we've looked at some other parts of the artist's language, you will have a chance to explore "dividing space" again on page 32.

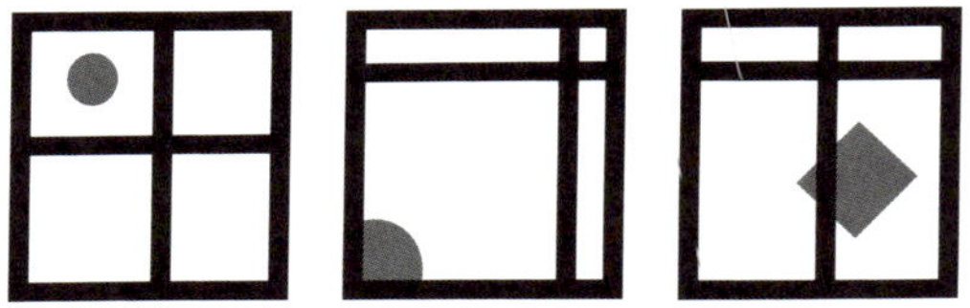

Art Choice

Draw a shape or shapes in different places in each of these boxes. Using lines, divide the rectangles in different ways. You can draw around or through your shapes. You may use as many lines as you would like.

Experiment Page

You will find **Experiment Pages** throughout this handbook. You can fill them in any way that you would like.

What happens when two lines meet? Turn the page.

Did you know that when two lines meet, they make a **shape**? Shapes are fun and easy to draw. They are an important part of the artist's language. There are two basic types of shapes: **geometric** and **biomorphic**.

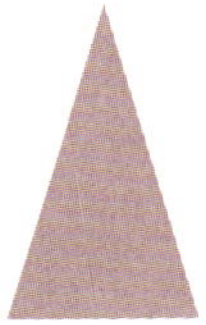

Geometric shapes are based on geometry. Examples include squares, rectangles, circles, triangles, and polygons. They often have more straight lines and angles.

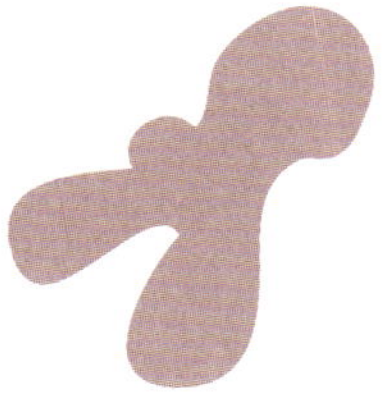

Biomorphic shapes are based on nature, such as animals or flowers, and often have more curved lines.

Which type of shape does Jacob Lawrence use in this painting from *The Migration Series?*

____

____

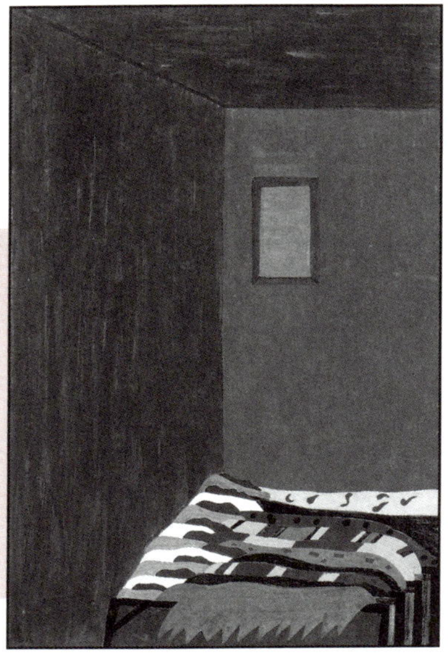

Jacob Lawrence, *The Migration Series, No. 47,* 1940–41.

The Shape of Things

Artists like to see things as shapes. When you draw something as a basic shape, you change it into something **abstract**. For example, a house could become a rectangle.

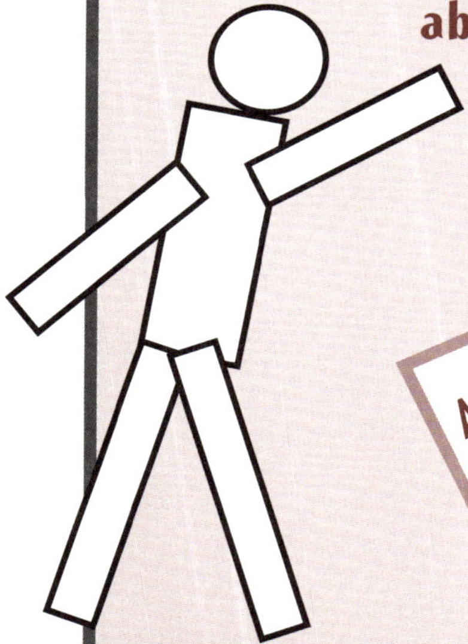

This drawing of a person walking is made out of five rectangles and a circle.

Art Choice

What could these abstract shapes be? Using lines and more shapes, transform each of these geometric shapes into something you can recognize, like a popsicle, a bike, or a person.

Experiment Page

I think of the content of my art as autobiographical.

Jacob **Lawrence**

Art Tip

Artists often start from another artist's drawing or painting idea.

Harlem *Home*

The Story of Jacob Lawrence

Many of Jacob Lawrence's early paintings are about home life. These paintings often take place in Harlem, the mostly African American community that Lawrence grew up in from the time he was 13. Look at the shapes that Lawrence painted in *The Homecoming* (painted when Lawrence was about 17).

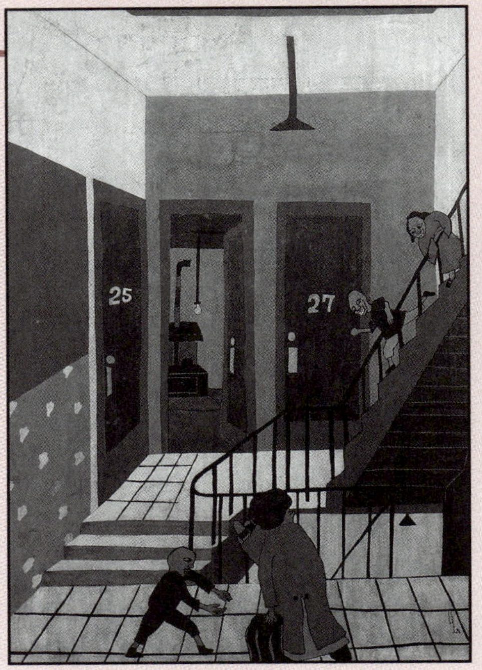

Jacob Lawrence, *The Homecoming*, 1936.

Art Choice

Artists like to draw from other artists. In the spaces below, draw some of the geometric shapes and biomorphic shapes (based on nature) that you see in Jacob Lawrence's painting called *The Homecoming*.

geometric shapes

biomorphic shapes

Sense of *Self*

The Shape of Home

Idea Starter

Filling in the blanks below might get you started with some ideas about your home.

When I am at home I feel ______________________

I would be happy if my home looked ______________________

My room can be (list three things)

1. ______________________
2. ______________________
3. ______________________

My favorite memory of being home is ______________________

My personal space at home is ______________________

Art Choice

Look for shapes at home. Choose some to draw in the space below. (They could be shapes that you see on your bed, through the windows, in the corner of a room, by a closet door, and more.)

geometric shapes

biomorphic shapes

Do you have a pattern? Do you go to school the same way every day? Talk on the phone a lot? Always hand in your homework late? Your DNA code is also your personal pattern. When you **repeat** a part of the artist's language like a line, shape, or color, you create an art pattern.

Jacob Lawrence enjoyed finding patterns everywhere. He especially liked the patterns he found in the rugs and quilts he saw at home as a child and in the buildings and fire escapes he saw in Harlem. He remembered these patterns and later used them in his paintings.

Art Choice

In each of these squares, two black circles have been drawn in the same place to create very different patterns. Using the two circles as a starting point, see if you can make two new patterns.

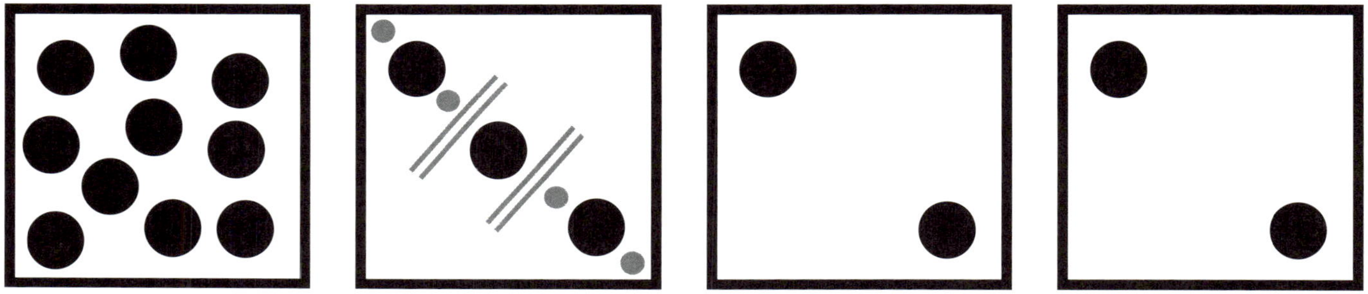

A pattern can seem **fast** or **slow**.

If there are many little things, a pattern will seem fast.
If there are a few big things, the pattern will seem slow.

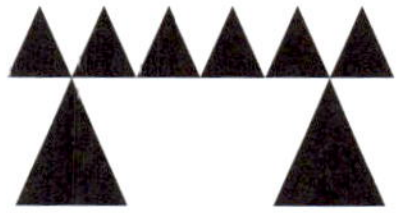

Things feel "fast" or "slow" because of the way your eyes see pattern, traveling from one shape to the next. This creates a **rhythm**. If there are many things to look at, your eyes move fast. If there are only a few things to look at your eyes move more slowly. We will talk more about rhythm later.

Art Choice

Try drawing a slow pattern and a fast pattern.

slow pattern

fast pattern

Harlem Neighborhood

The Story of Jacob Lawrence

> For recreation I used to walk the streets of the community of Harlem.
>
> I would leave the Apollo Theater, go out on the street and it was like a continuation of what was going on the stage.
>
> Jacob **Lawrence**

Jacob Lawrence's neighborhood **inspired** his art. He looked closely at many things in his **environment**. He enjoyed observing the patterns of the fire escapes, street performers, and theater, including the funny performers in vaudeville who spoofed everyday life.

Lawrence also painted and drew things that he didn't like about his environment. Why might you, as an artist, paint a picture about something you don't like in your neighborhood? Lawrence felt that making pictures of difficult parts of life helped him feel that he was more in control of those things.

Art Choice

Look at Lawrence's *Play Street*, which he painted when he was in his twenties. Notice the different things that Lawrence tells us about his neighborhood in this painting: the patterns of buildings, storefronts, and people at play.

In the boxes below, draw some of the patterns that Lawrence used to describe this summer scene of children playing in a sprinkler.

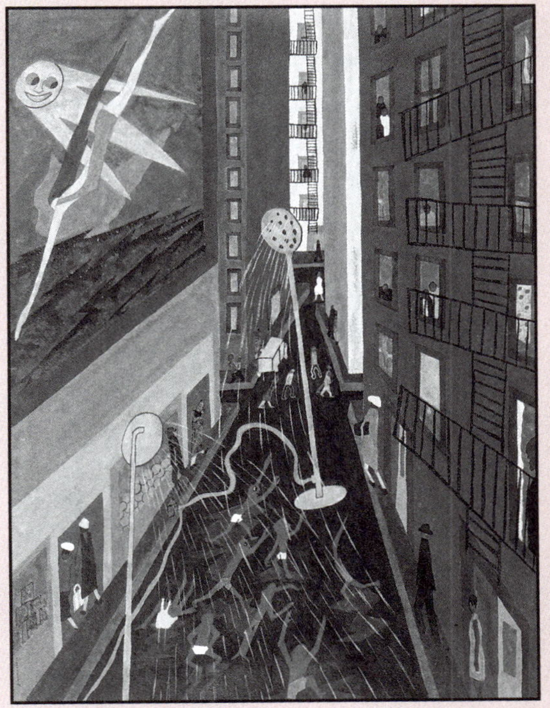

Jacob Lawrence, *Play Street*, 1942

Sense of *Self*

Neighborhood Know-how

Art Choice

Now that you've studied Jacob Lawrence's neighborhood patterns, look for some near you. In the boxes below, draw three different art patterns that you see in your neighborhood (for example: buildings, architectural details like windows and doors, street lines, street signs, billboards, people walking, crowds, cars lined up on the street, buses, people waiting for the bus in the morning). Use an "experiment page" if you need more space or would like to make more patterns.

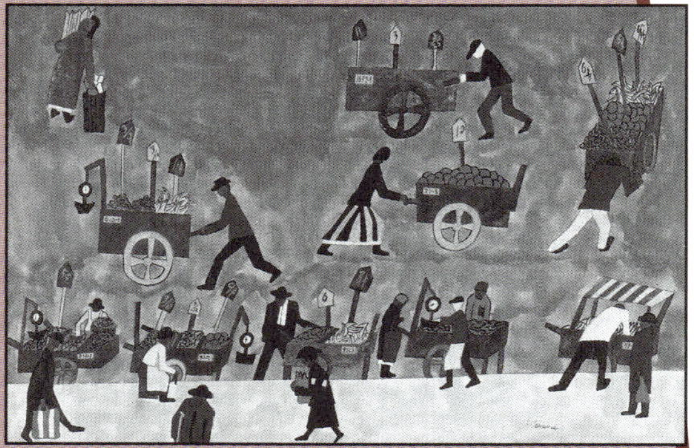

Jacob Lawrence, *Peddlers Reduce Their Prices in the Evening to Get Rid of Their Perishables,* 1943.

Idea Starter

How do you feel about your neighborhood? Filling in the blanks below might get you started with some ideas.

Name two things you like about your neighborhood.

____

____

Name two things you would like to change in your neighborhood.

____

____

Name two places that are important to you in your neighborhood (for example, the CD store, the playground, or a special friend's house — be specific).

____

____

Name two people from your neighborhood (for example, neighbors, friends, or other characters).

____

____

Name two things you like to do in your neighborhood.

____

____

Experiment Page

Pattern

Turn the page to see how a shape can "go" 3-D!

How Can You Make Something Look 3-D?

Some artists like to give their shapes drama, energy, and zing by using shades of **light** and **dark**. When artists draw shapes of light and dark they often use the artist's term **value**, which just means how the artist applies white, black, and grays.

The more shades of light and dark you add to a shape, the more the shape will look **3-D** (three-dimensional), like you could reach out and pick it up. Another way of saying something looks 3-D is to say that it has **volume**.

With less shading, we see two shapes.

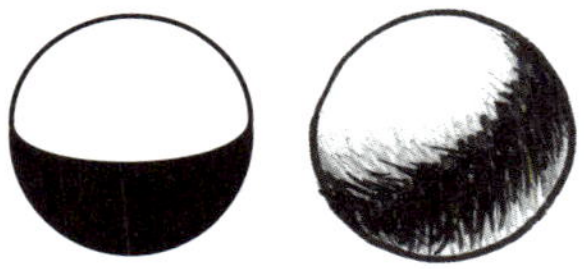

With more shading (changes from light to dark) the circle looks 3-D.

Of course it all depends on where your **light source** is. In this diagram you can see that certain things always happen: there's always a light side, a dark side, and a cast shadow. These are good things to know.

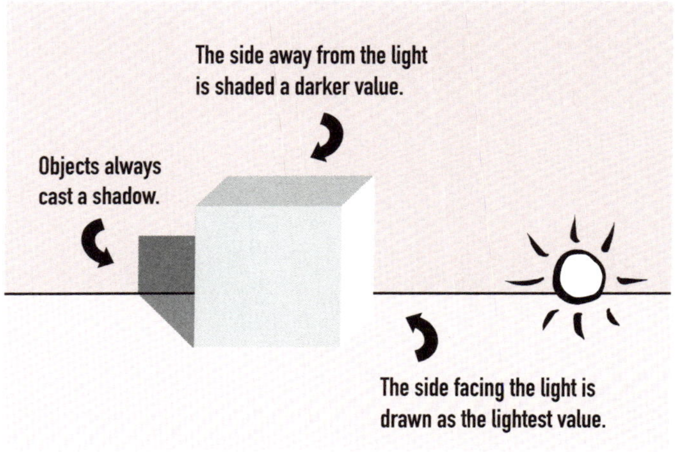

Art Choice

Try shading these shapes to make them look 3-D. Tip: The light source (the sun in this case) is in a different place each time. Make sure to also shade in each object's shadow.

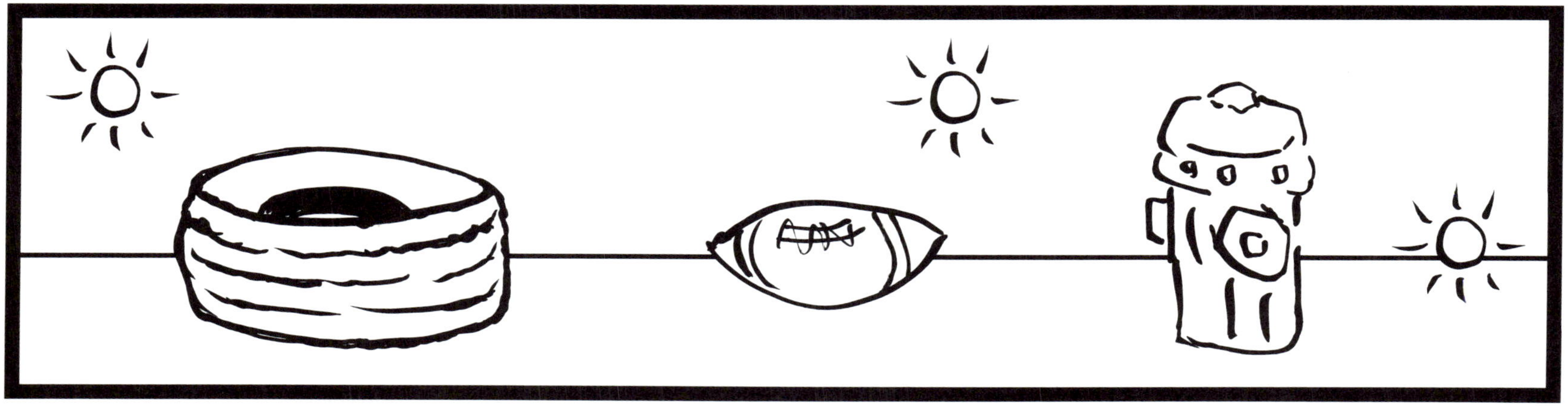

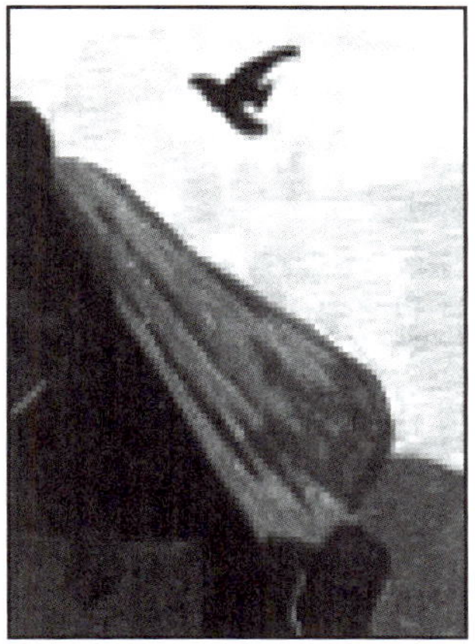

Study this detail from *The Migration Series, No. 3*. (Look at page 9 to see the whole painting.) How does Jacob Lawrence make this sack look 3-D? Try to draw it on the experiment page.

Art Choice

Artists who are successful **practice**. Try shading in Lawrence's line drawing to practice.

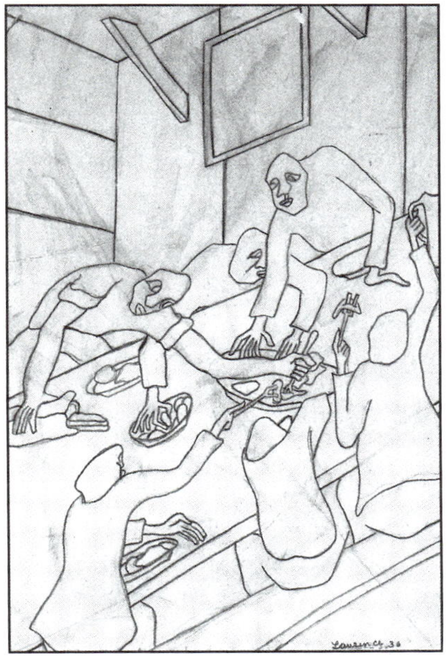

Jacob Lawrence, *Chow*, 1936.

Experiment Page

Workshop

The Story of Jacob Lawrence

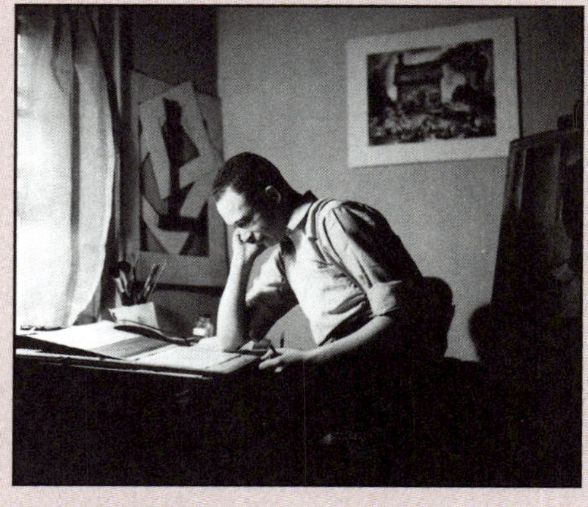

Charles Alston, 1930s.

The African American artist and teacher Charles Alston became Lawrence's first **mentor** and **role model**. This didn't happen over night. When he was a teenager, Jacob Lawrence attended after-school arts programs in Harlem. Alston was the teacher in charge of this after-school program. (See the chapter called "Workshop" in *I See You, I See Myself* to learn more about this period in Lawrence's life.)

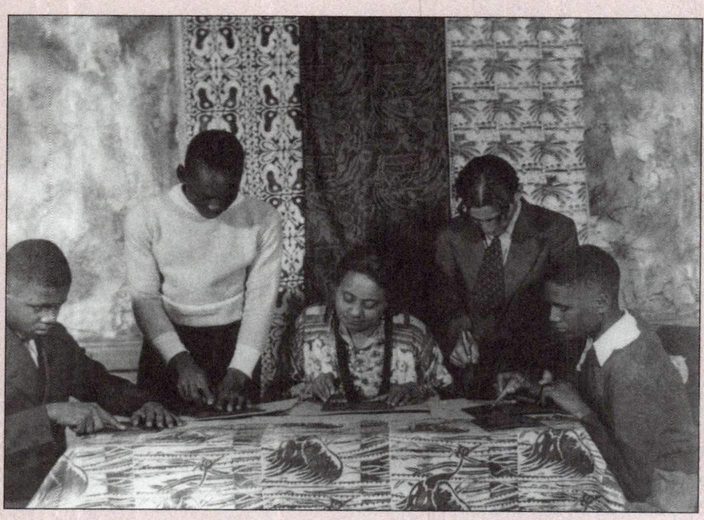

Jacob Lawrence (second from left) making block prints in the Harlem art workshop, c. 1933–34.

As Lawrence's mentor, Alston **encouraged** the young artist to make his own **choices**. Lawrence would often have an idea about what he wanted as his subject, for example, things he saw in his neighborhood or in his home. Instead of forcing his own ideas on Lawrence, Alston guided the young art student by teaching him the artist's language (the same way that you are learning in this handbook). He also gave him a variety of materials to use and encouraged Lawrence to **experiment**.

Sense of *Self*

Having Heroes

Idea Starter

Who do you look up to?

Name three famous people who you would like to have lunch with. (They can be from the past or the present.)

1. ______________________
2. ______________________
3. ______________________

Name three people you know or have known who you'd like to have lunch with.

1. ______________________
2. ______________________
3. ______________________

Name three people who are important to you and are part of your neighborhood or community (for example, a teacher, minister, family member, or neighbor).

1. ______________________
2. ______________________
3. ______________________

Pick one of the people you listed and write an imaginary postcard to him or her, introducing yourself. Include two or three things about yourself that you described in your "idea starters." What question would you ask this person if you could? Use an "experiment page" if you need more space.

Using Light and Dark to Create Balance

Artists are like tight-rope walkers. If a tight-rope walker loses his **balance**, he falls. We lose interest after he hits the net. If an artist's picture isn't balanced, the artist doesn't fall, but the picture fails to keep our interest.

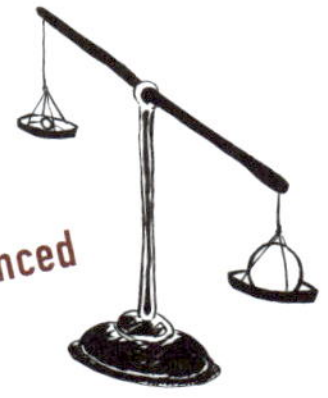

Jacob Lawrence, like other artists, wants to keep you looking at his pictures. If a work is balanced you want to keep looking at it. If a work of art is unbalanced, your eyes are more likely to leave the picture fast! There are three ways to balance a picture.

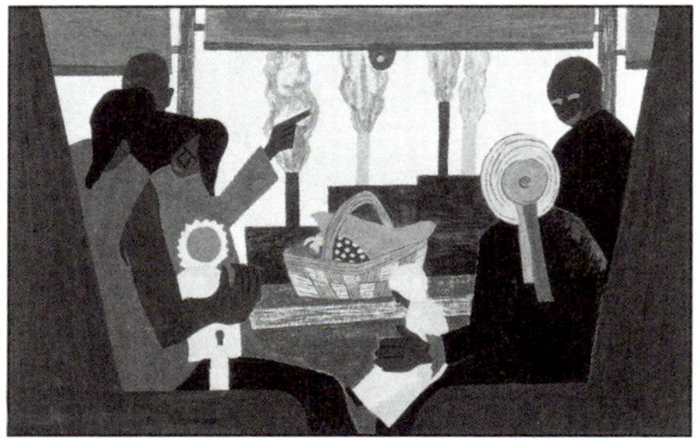

Jacob Lawrence, *The Migration Series, No. 45*, 1940–41.

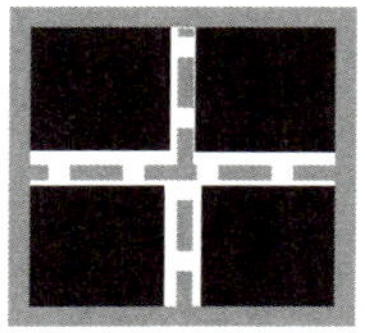

radial

It looks the same from all sides.

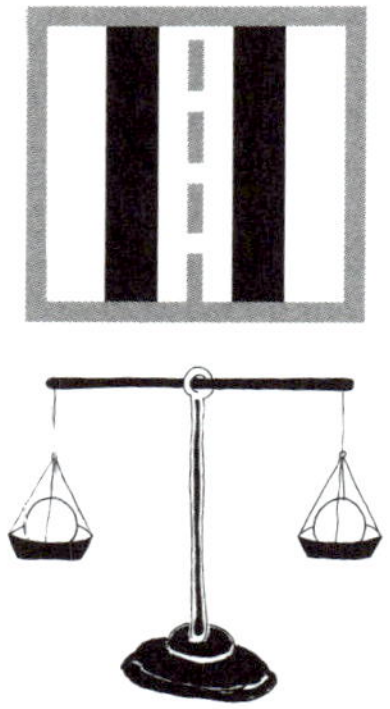

symmetrical

If you divided it down the middle, it would pretty much be the same on both sides (like standing with both feet on the ground).

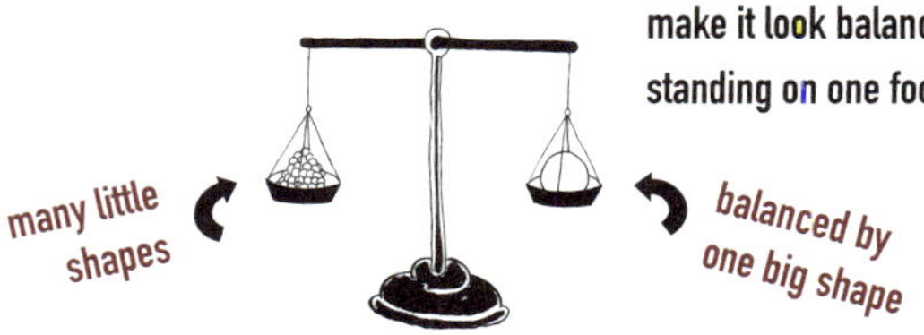

asymmetrical

The left and the right are not the same, but other things like the size, shape, color, and value make it look balanced (like standing on one foot).

Art Choice

What kind of balance did Jacob Lawrence use in the painting above? ______________________

Try creating your own balanced pictures. In the rectangles below, draw shapes of light and dark to make these **compositions**.

Create a *symmetrical* composition.

Create a *radial* composition.

Create an *asymmetrical* composition.

Color

At last, we have arrived at **color**! Color is an exciting part of the artist's language. Using colors can be fun and spontaneous. There are a lot of interesting things to learn about color too. **Hue** is the artist's word for the color of the paint. You can do a lot with one hue by adding white and black to lighten or darken it.

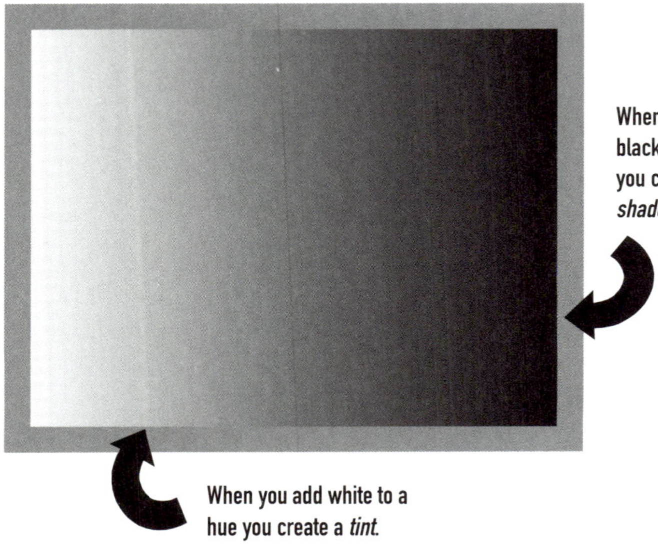

When you add black to a hue you create a *shade.*

When you add white to a hue you create a *tint.*

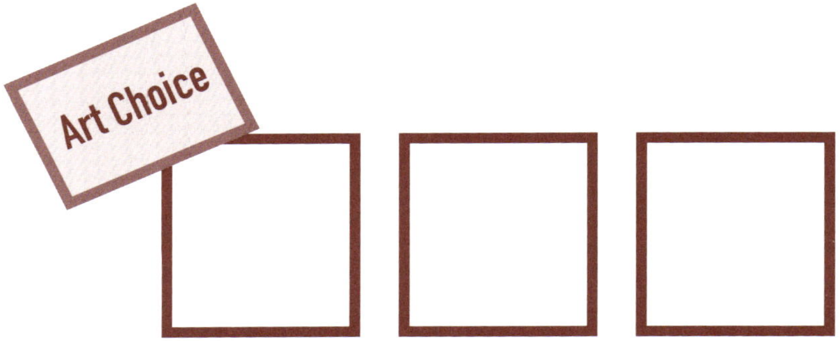

In the boxes above, experiment with **tints** and **shades**. Use one colored pencil plus a black pencil to create a shade. How could you use a colored pencil and the white of the paper to create a tint?

The **primary colors** are red, yellow, and blue. The primary colors are important because all other colors can be mixed from them. If you were an artist on a desert island, you would want red, yellow, and blue paints.

On the color wheel, when you mix two primary colors, you get a **secondary color**.

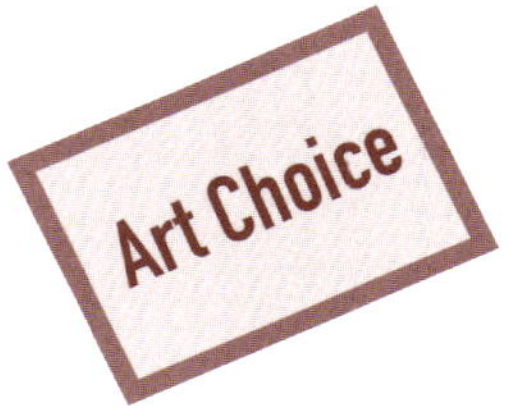

Create a world of color by filling in the color wheel with colored pencils or markers.

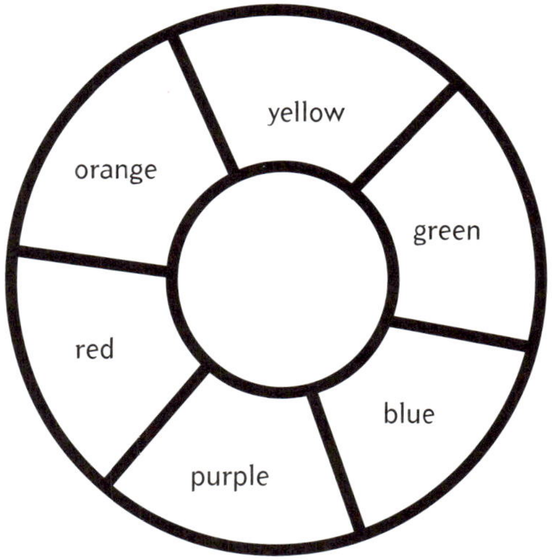

Art Tip

Less Is *More*

Jacob Lawrence liked to use the primary and secondary colors. At first he only used these colors because he couldn't afford many paints. But later, he made the **choice** to use very few colors. When you use fewer colors it creates **unity**. Unity means that things look like they go together, like matching clothes or singing in unison.

Art Choice

If you could only choose three colors, which colors would you select? The primaries? The secondaries? Others?

1. ______________________
2. ______________________
3. ______________________

Using *only* the colors you selected above, fill in the Jacob Lawrence line drawing at the right to create a picture with unity.

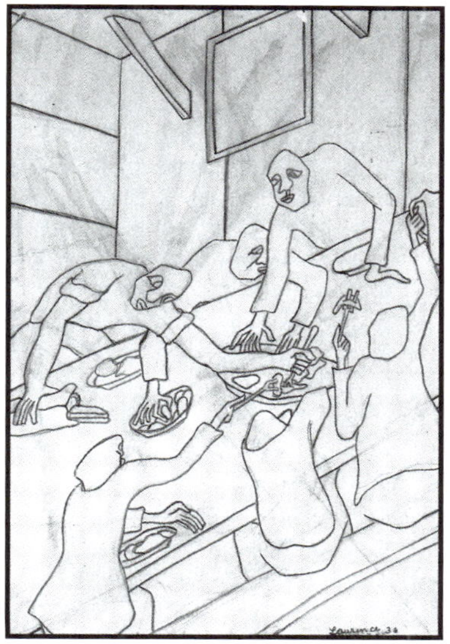

Jacob Lawrence, *Chow,* 1936.

Complementary colors are special pairs of colors. When they are placed next to each other, pairs of complementary colors *complement* each other: They make each other look brighter. All colors have a complement. You can find complementary color pairs easily on the color wheel; a color's complement is always directly across from it.

Can you find a painting by Jacob Lawrence in *I See You, I See Myself* where he uses a complementary color pair?

____

Some Complementary Color Pairs:

RED & green
blue & ORANGE
YELLOW & purple

Art Choice

If you could only choose one complementary color pair, which one would you select? Write in the colors here.

1. ______________________
2. ______________________

Using *only* the complementary colors you selected above, fill in the Jacob Lawrence line drawing at the right to create a picture with unity.

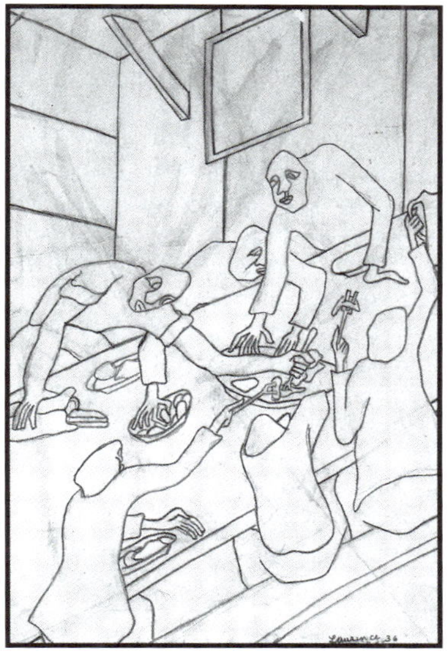

Jacob Lawrence, *Chow,* 1936.

The Color of *Feelings*

Colors can stir up strong feelings. For example, some people say, "He's seeing red," when they mean, "He's angry."

Look at the color drawings you made on the previous page. Do both drawings make you feel the same way? Does the color affect how you feel about the drawing? How so? For example, does one set of colors make the picture seem happier or sadder to you?

Art Choice

Artists use color on purpose to communicate their feelings to you. Find a painting by Jacob Lawrence in *I See You, I See Myself* that gives you:

the feeling of anger: ______________________

the feeling of excitement:

____

Try experimenting with different color combinations and the feelings they give you in the space below.

Idea Starter

In each blank, write in a color that seems to match the feeling. Remember, there is no "correct" answer.

When he saw something that made him angry, he would see ______________.
(anger)

She was so ______________ about the
(jealous?)
other girls that she could get ______________.
(sad)

Every day after school he was as ______________
(excited)
as he was ______________ to be out of class.
(happy)

306 was part of my education where I came into contact with older people, talking about their challenges in their art.

Jacob **Lawrence**

Around Town

Friends at 306

The Story of Jacob Lawrence

Charles Alston, Lawrence's mentor, thought of art as a serious profession, one that Lawrence should consider.

Alston belonged to a group of African American artists who had a **bodega** called "306" Studio. (Because it was at 306 West 141st Street.) Alston introduced Lawrence to many of the artists there.

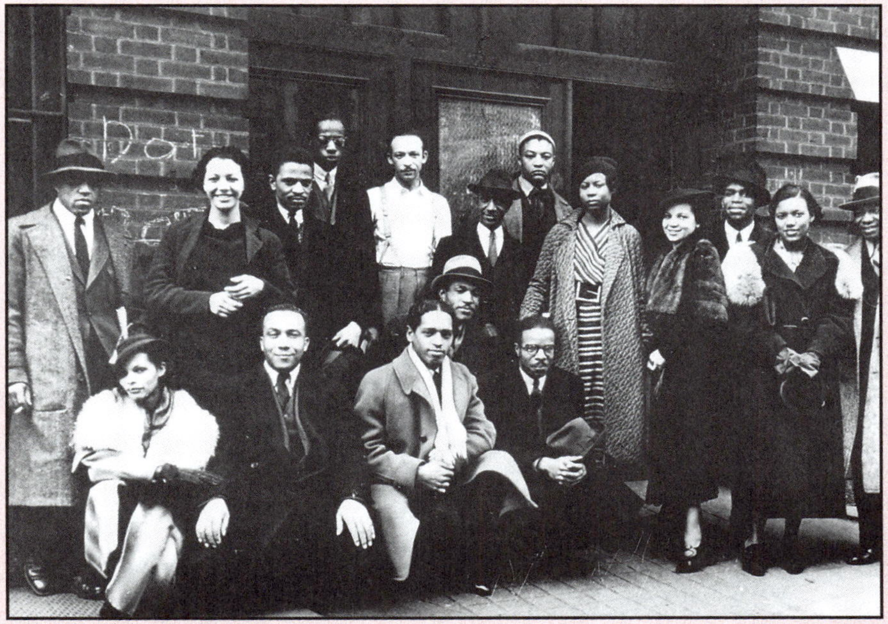

Artists of "306" Studio, late 1930s.

A bodega is a place where artists who work in different art forms share **studio** space. In the studio, they create and talk about their work: painting, printmaking, sculpture, dance, music, poetry, literature, and drama.

Lawrence was excited by the way the artists, poets, musicians, playwrights, and actors all used a similar **artist's language** to talk about their work and the problems they were facing in it.

Looking Again at Dividing Space

Now that you have experimented with all of the elements in the artist's language—line, shape, light and dark, color, and pattern—it is fun to look again at interesting and creative ways to divide the space in the picture.

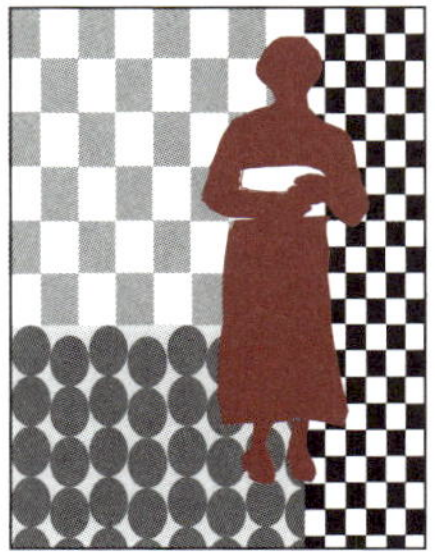

Art Choice

Jacob Lawrence often used **patterns** to **divide space**. In the boxes below, create two or three patterns and place them around each figure in some way. You can draw the patterns or you can cut them out of magazines or newspapers.

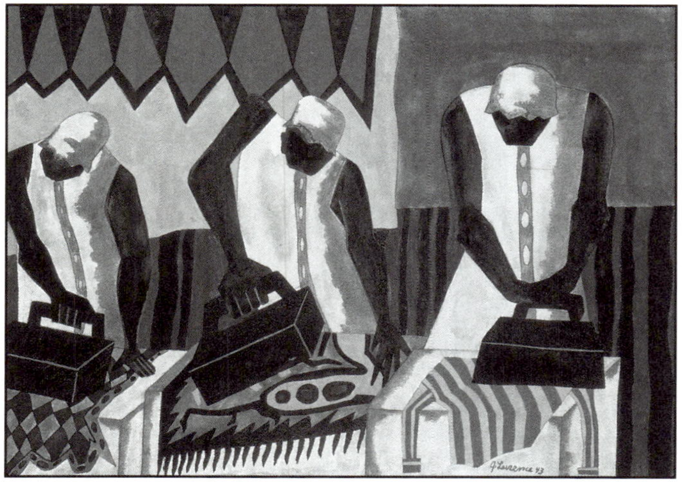

Jacob Lawrence, *Ironers*, 1943.

How many patterns did Jacob Lawrence use to divide space in *Ironers*?__________________

Some artists like to create an **illusion** in their paintings and drawings. The illusion is that a piece of paper or a canvas can look like a space that you can actually step into. That is to say that it looks like a **3-D space** or that it has **depth**.

On the following page are some artist's techniques to help you create the illusion of 3-D space on a piece of paper. Jacob Lawrence thought it was **magical** to see how artists could create the illusion of space. It was one of his favorite things to look for in paintings at the Metropolitan Museum of Art in New York.

These are three tricks that you can use to make a shape *look* like it is farther back in **space**:

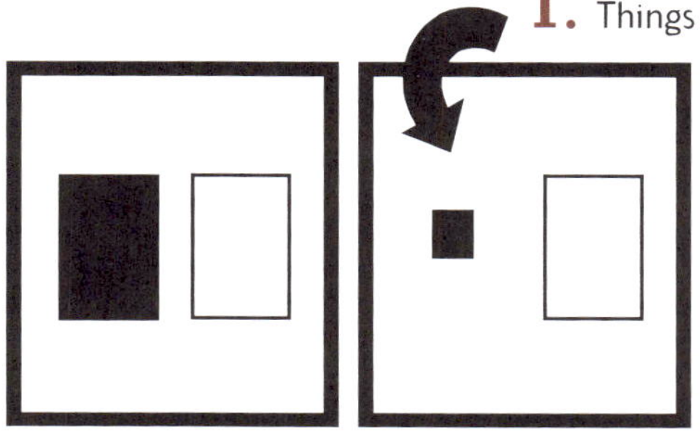

1. Things that are **smaller** appear to be farther away. Things that are **darker** also appear to be farther away.

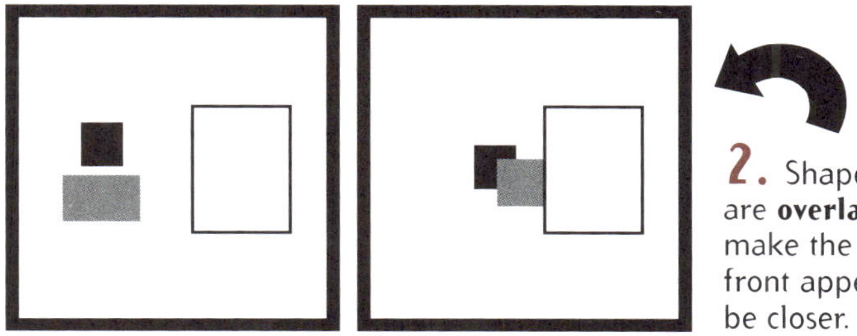

2. Shapes that are **overlapped** make the one in front appear to be closer.

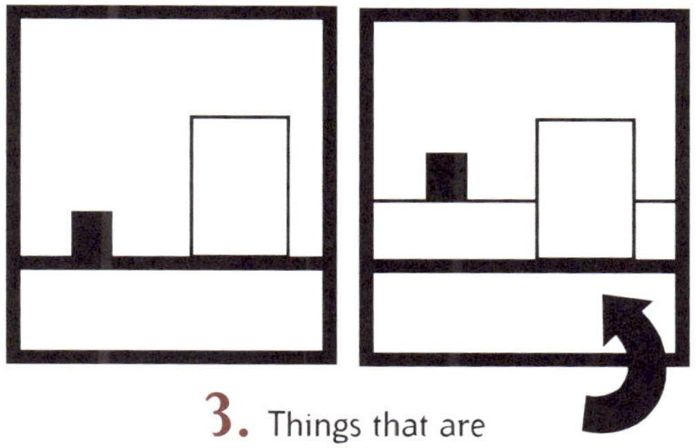

3. Things that are **higher** in the picture seem to be farther away.

Getting Perspective

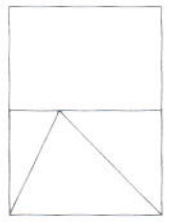

Another way that artists create the illusion of depth is with a system called **perspective**. To learn more about perspective, ask your art teacher.

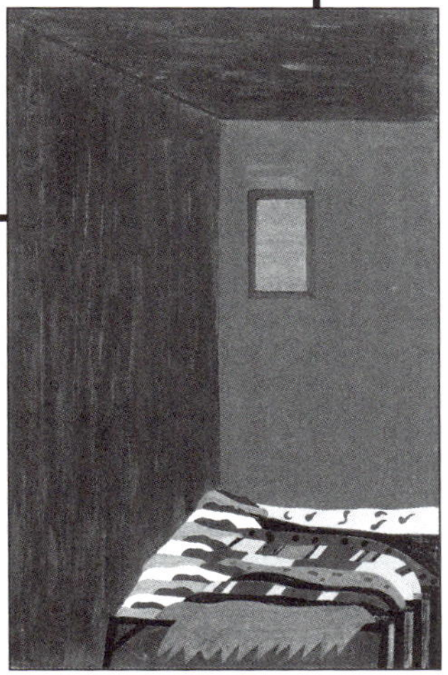

Jacob Lawrence, *The Migration Series, No. 47,* 1940-41.

Art Choice

Add a tree to this picture. Make your tree look like it is in the **distance**.

How big will you draw it?

Where will it go?

Up top? Down below?

Will it overlap the other tree?

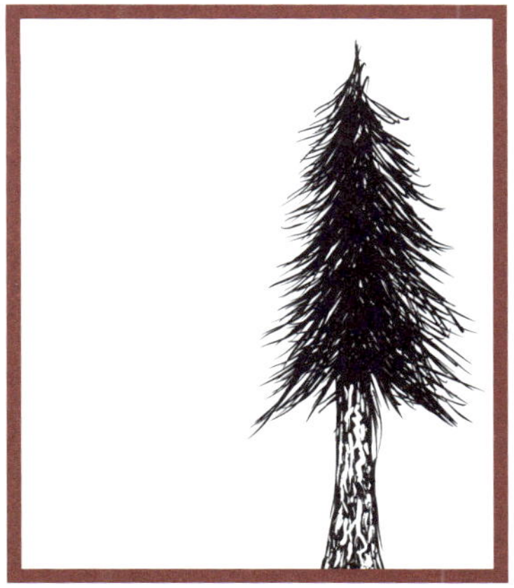

Art Choice

Try this pattern versus depth experiment. Using the same shapes, make a flat pattern in one square and create a picture of depth in the other.

Around Town

Personal Space

The Story of Jacob Lawrence

At "306" Studio, Jacob Lawrence not only met other artists, but Charles Alston even rented a corner of his studio, his art space, to the young art student. This was Lawrence's first personal space to be a serious artist. It was very important to him. He was 17.

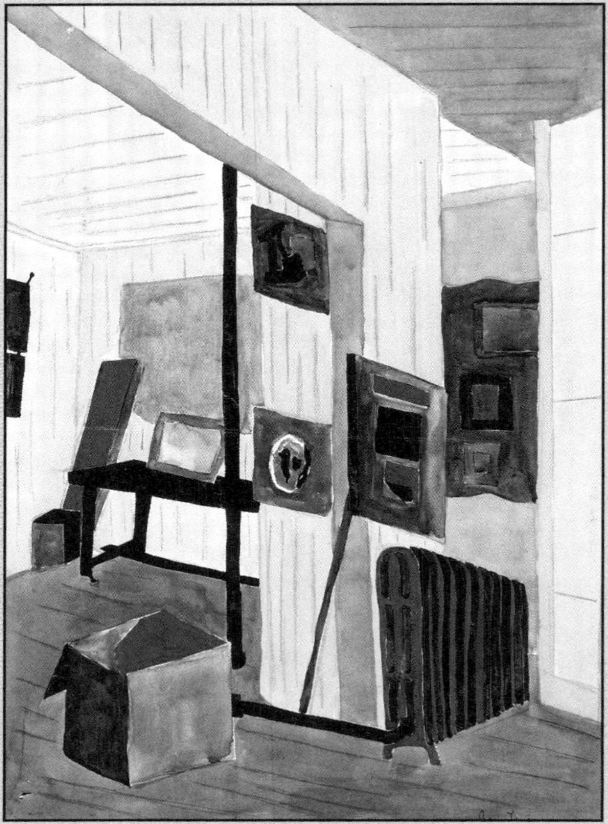

Jacob Lawrence, *Studio Corner,* 1936.

Sense of *Self*

Personal Space

Idea Starter

Where is your personal space?

____

Describe how your personal space looks. How do you mark this space as yours? Posters? A bulletin board?

____

____

____

____

____

____

____

____

How do you mark where your personal space begins?

____

____

____

Around Town

Seeing New Sights

The Story of Jacob Lawrence

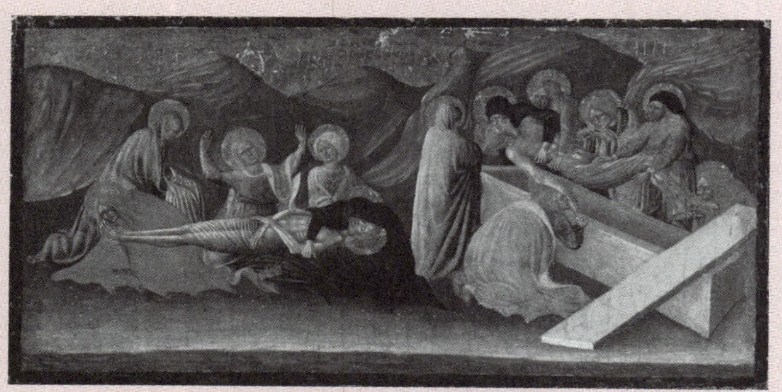

Bartolomeo di Tommaso, *The Lamentation and the Entombment*
The Metropolitan Museum of Art, Gwynne Andrews Fund, 1958. (58.87.2)
Photograph © 1988 The Metropolitan Museum of Art

Lawrence and his friends from "306" (including the artist Gwendolyn Knight whom he would later marry) thought it was extremely important for artists to see other kinds of art outside Harlem.

They went to **gallery** exhibitions downtown where they saw some of the **new** art being created.

They went to **museums** to see art of the **past** from different periods in history.

Charles Alston emphasized that it was important to look at many different sources, from Italian Renaissance painting to African sculpture.

Art Choice

Look for Lawrence's *sources* in his paintings. After looking at the painting by Bartolomeo di Tommaso at the top of this page and the African sculpture at the right, find paintings by Jacob Lawrence that might have been influenced by these sources. (There are no wrong answers.)

Painting that might have been influenced by *The Lamentation and the Entombment:*

____

Painting that might have been influenced by African sculpture:

____

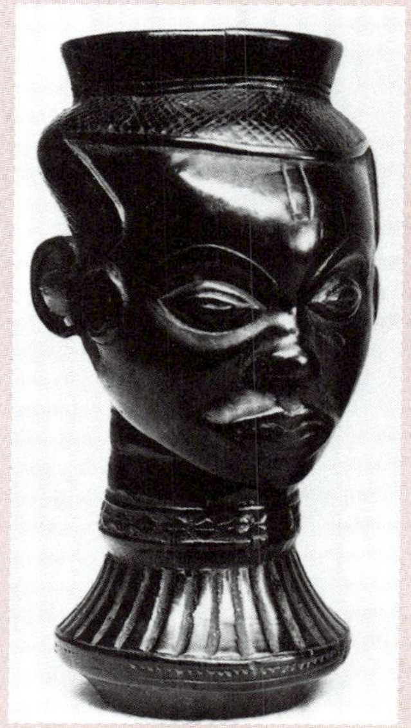

Goblet in the form of a human head, Zaïre, Musée de l'Homme, Paris
Photograph © Musée de l'Homme

Jacob Lawrence saw this sculpture in an important exhibition of African art at the Museum of Modern Art in 1935.

Experiment Page

Art Choice

Pick one of the pictures from the previous page or find a postcard of a work of art that you have seen. Choose something that you like about it and draw it on this "experiment page." Do you like its lines, shapes, colors, or a particular pattern? Your drawing doesn't have to look like the artwork you selected.

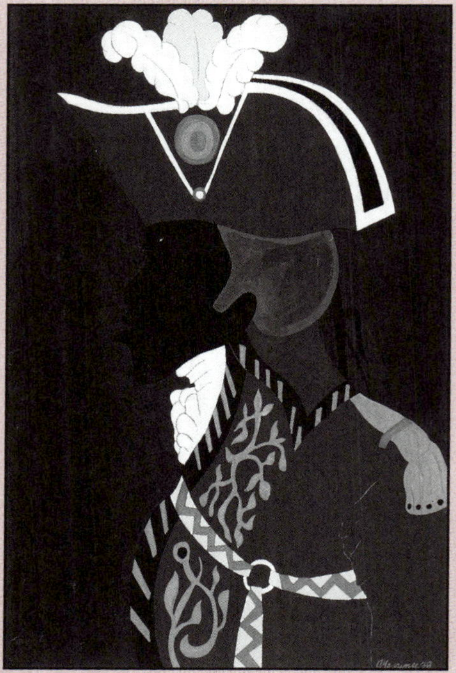

Jacob Lawrence, ***The Life of Toussaint L'Ouverture, No. 20,*** **1938.**

Downtown

from Harlem to History

The Story of Jacob Lawrence

Jacob Lawrence liked to go to the **theaters** in Harlem. The performances he saw were important **sources** for his paintings. When he was 18, he saw a play thought, mistakenly, to be by the famous African American writer W. E. B. Dubois. It was about the black hero Toussaint L'Ouverture (say *too-sant low-va-chure*), who helped to liberate the Caribbean nation of Haiti, which became the first black republic in the Western Hemisphere.

Idea Starter

Name 3 things you'd like to change about the world.

1. ______________________________

2. ______________________________

3. ______________________________

Jacob Lawrence was **inspired**. He wanted to create a group of paintings about Toussaint L'Ouverture. He went to the **library** to find out more about him. After completing *The Life of Toussaint L'Ouverture*, which was exhibited at the Baltimore Museum of Art, Lawrence was considered a newly "discovered" artist.

In the next three years he made several groups of paintings about African American heroes, including Harriet Tubman and Frederick Douglass.

Like his fellow artists at "306" Studio, Lawrence believed that the African American story needed to be told. He felt that the story of African Americans was invisible to white America. He wanted to raise **awareness**. Lawrence hoped that, by looking at his pictures, people might see something in a new way or for the first time—like the racism he faced or the struggles and triumphs of African American heroes and everyday people.

Sense of *Self*

The Drama of History

Idea Starter

Describe a TV show (episode), a play, or a movie that you like. Why do you like it?

Idea Starter

Have you ever felt invisible? Like no one cared about what you were doing, feeling, or thinking? Describe an experience.

Idea Starter

Name 3 people from history who you like.

1.
2.
3.

What do art and music have in common? Turn the page.

One of the words that Lawrence probably heard discussed at "306" was **rhythm**. As already discussed, rhythm in a painting can be created through repeated **patterns**. Of course, a piece of **music** or poetry has rhythm too.

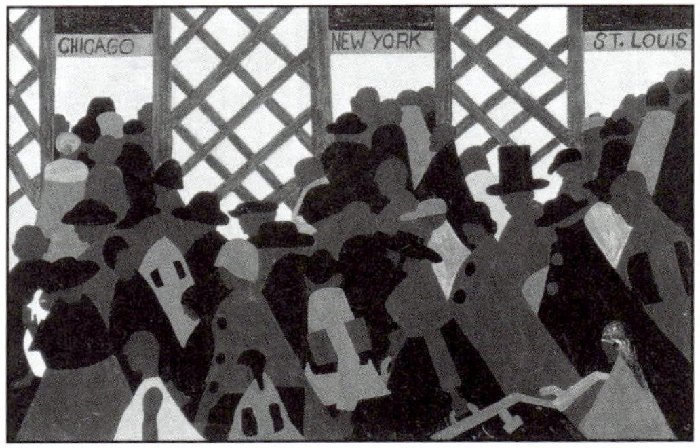

Jacob Lawrence, *The Migration Series, No. 1*, 1940–41.

When you clap your hands repeatedly, you create a rhythm.
When you snap your fingers repeatedly, you create a rhythm.
When you walk down the street, you create a rhythm.
When you draw a series of lines, you create a rhythm.

Art Choice

Draw a series of lines and shapes in the following rhythms. Remember, longer, bigger, and fewer lines and shapes seem to go more slowly. Smaller and more numerous lines and shapes seem to go faster.

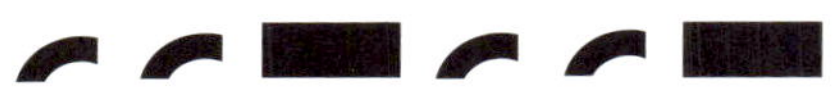

quick, quick, slow, quick, quick, slow

slow, quick, slow, quick, slow, slow, slow

slow, quick, quick, slow, quick, quick

How does a musician or a composer **divide space**?

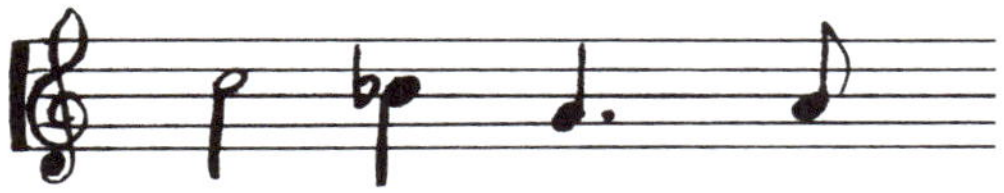

The composer divides time and sounds when he writes music in a score like the one above. The order of each note shows when it is to be played; the placement of each note on the horizontal lines shows what *tone* should be played; and the shape and color of each note show how long it should be played.

Art Choice

Listen to a **favorite song**. In the box here or on an "experiment page," draw the **rhythms** that you hear.

Art and **poetry** can be fun to link. Langston Hughes was a famous African American poet. Jacob Lawrence knew him, and in fact, Hughes asked Lawrence to illustrate his poem called "One-Way Ticket," which you can read on the next page. As you read "One-Way Ticket," which, like *The Migration Series*, is about moving, consider some of these "art links."

Write a line from "One-Way Ticket" that Langston Hughes repeats to create a **pattern** and **rhythm**.

____

Why do you think that he **repeats** this line? ____

Look at the way that Langston Hughes **divides space**. Reread the poem and notice when you have to look to the next line. (Looking to the next line makes you pause for a split second.)

Art Choice

In the rectangle, create a pattern with lines and shapes based on "One-Way Ticket." Will it be fast? Slow? Have different rhythms? Will it be colorful? Will it be dull?

We have talked about some of the ways that color can give you a **feeling**. Artists who work in all art forms from painting to poetry also show their feelings in their work. They often talk about creating a **mood** in their work.

What do you think the mood of "One-Way Ticket" is? (circle)

HAPPY SAD ANGRY EXCITED SOMETHING ELSE: ________________________

Write a line from the poem that shows this mood: ________________________

How does the rhythm show this mood? Does it flow gently; is it harsh; is it halting? ________________________

Can you find a painting by Jacob Lawrence that seems to have the same mood? ________________________

One-Way Ticket

by Langston Hughes, 1948

I pick up my life
And take it with me
And I put it down in
Chicago, Detroit,
Buffalo, Scranton,
Any place that is
North and East—
And not Dixie.

I pick up my life
And take it on the train
To Los Angeles, Bakersfield,
Seattle, Oakland, Salt Lake,
Any place that is
North and West—
But not South.

I am fed up
With Jim Crow laws,
People who are cruel
And afraid.

Who lynch and run,
Who are scared of me
And me of them.

I pick up my life
And take it away
On a one-way ticket—
Gone up North,
Gone out West,
Gone!

Experiment Page

Art Choice

Jacob Lawrence turned theater into art. Now see if you can turn art into theater! Select a painting by Lawrence with at least two people in it.

Name of the painting:

____

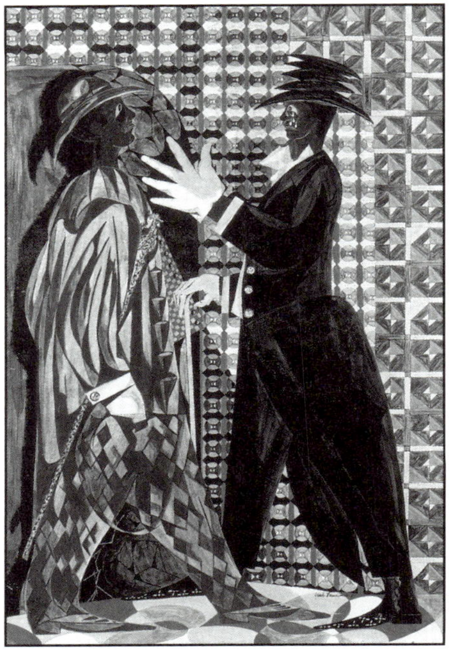

Jacob Lawrence, *Vaudeville,* 1951.

Transform this painting into a scene from a **play**.

Describe the character in this painting. In the space provided below, step into that **character's shoes**.

Describe what it's like to be *this* person in *this* painting.

What do you see?

What do you hear?

What do you smell?

How do you feel?

What are you thinking or saying?

Art Choice

Using the character you just wrote about, create a **dialogue**, a conversation between two characters. How does the dialogue create a **mood**? Are the characters fighting? Are they playing? What are they saying?

Character 1:

Character 2:

Character 1:

Character 2:

Character 1:

Character 2:

What Does Your "Path" Look Like?

Looking at your "idea starters" in this handbook, describe different characteristics of yourself in each of the shapes. Write, draw, or consider pasting in photos or clippings. Add more shapes or fill up the whole sheet! Use "experiment pages" if you need more space.

describe yourself! from the outside

height: ____________

hair color: ____________

skin color: ____________

eye color: ____________

shape: ____________

describe yourself! from the inside

- Describe one of your happiest moments.

- How do you deal with struggle and difficult situations? For example, what do you do when you are looked down on, or when you don't get what you want? Smile, get tough, get weepy? Describe.

Fill in the blanks
to describe yourself.

favorite color: ______________

favorite place: ________________

a sound you like: ________________

a sound you don't like: ________________

favorite holiday: ____________________

favorite artist: ____________________

favorite musical group: ____________

favorite food: ________________

a food you don't like: ________

More Ideas

- Create a logo of yourself. (Use your initials or a flower or animal that you like a lot.)
- Paste in photos of your friends and family members.
- Paste in a baby picture of yourself.
- Draw in a family tree.
- Take photographs or draw sketches of your neighborhood.

Imagine Your *Future*

What kind of job do you have?
Where are you living?
Who are your friends?
Describe.

Art Start

What's Your Personal Style?

Do you dress in a certain way? Fix your hair in a special way? Listen to particular kinds of music? Walk a certain way? This is your style.

Artists also have personal art styles. This happens over time after looking at different kinds of art, experimenting with the artist's language, and practicing. You can sometimes recognize an artist's style the way you recognize someone's handwriting.

The Style of Jacob Lawrence

Jacob Lawrence's style is easy to spot.

lines: lots of diagonals, often clear outline
color: bright; rarely mixes colors, uses a limited number for each painting
shapes: simplified abstract shapes, often geometric; paints with flat shapes of color
light and dark: uses to create pattern
pattern: uses it a lot
balance: both symmetrical and asymmetrical
space: uses overlapping shapes to show depth
subjects: everyday life, the history of African Americans
sources: memories of childhood surroundings and experiences in Harlem, works by other artists, African art, theater, history

Your Art Style (so far)

Follow this **art questionnaire** to determine your art style. Your style is made up of the things that you like.

Look through your handbook to choose the following things:

Subjects

Looking through your "idea starters," list three subjects that you might like to make into an art project.

1. ______________________________

2. ______________________________

3. ______________________________

Sources

What are your sources for subjects and inspiration?
(Check off as many as you like.)

☐ your surroundings (home, neighborhood)
☐ your experiences
☐ your memories
☐ works by other artists
☐ history
☐ music
☐ plays, TV, movies
☐ poetry
☐ fiction

Favorite Kind of Line:

Favorite Color(s):

Favorite Shape(s):

Favorite Way of Dividing Space:

Favorite Pattern:

Turn the page to start an art project!

Now that you have a sense of your art style, try it out! Artists often select a topic they'd like to **explore** in several works of art (for example: trees, cows, the Civil War, American cities, the color yellow). Some artists work in **series**, where there is some sort of link from one artwork to the next.

Art Start

Select one of the subjects you chose as part of your "art style."

Subject: ____

After you've selected your subject, start to **brainstorm**. Do this by doodling on an "experiment page." Write down or draw three things about your subject.

What does it look like?

How does it make you feel?

If it could talk, what would it say?

Let your mind return to your memories. See what happens . . .

Art Start

Create a series of three drawings about this subject. Jacob Lawrence often considered **point of view** in his series paintings. He would change the **size** of his subject, and experiment with **close-ups**. Make a progression; for example, in one picture draw a flower seen from close-up and in another, a flower seen from far away.

1 **2** **3**

From Poster Paints to Clay

It's fun to think about doing the same project but with different **materials**.

As a teenager, Jacob Lawrence liked to experiment with all sorts of materials. Here are some of the things he used that you could use too. You could:

- Paint with tempera paints (poster paints).
- Make a stage set. Use a shoe box to create a stage. Create scenery and cut out characters with tabs to fit into the bottom of the box. Cut slits in the bottom of the box for the tabs.
- Make a block print. With an adult's supervision, carve a design in the end of a potato that has been cut in half, or in a gum eraser. Create your own stamp pad. Put a damp paper towel in a dish. Put a little tempera paint on the damp towel and stamp.
- Sculpt with clay. You could use Playdough, Sculpee, or even crumpled-up paper.

Do You Like Comics?

In his early 20s, Jacob Lawrence created series that were also **stories**.

A **narrative** is another word for story. Comic strips are probably one of the most popular forms of narrative art. Like comics, Lawrence gave each painting in his series a **caption** describing the scene. Here are four panels from Lawrence's *Migration Series*, 1940-41 (there are 60 panels altogether). Look at the panels to get a sense of the meaning of the story. Now read the captions. Does it change how you think about the story?

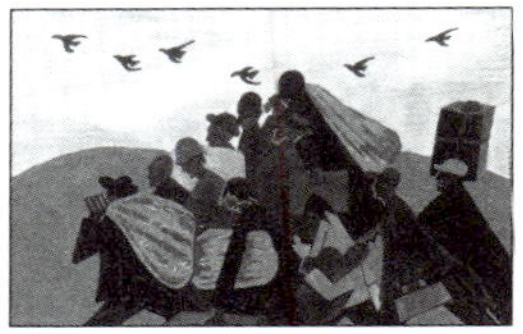

No. 3
From every southern town migrants left by the hundreds to travel north.

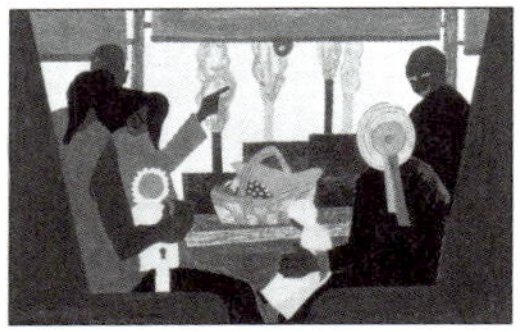

No. 45
The migrants arrived in Pittsburgh, one of the great industrial centers of the North.

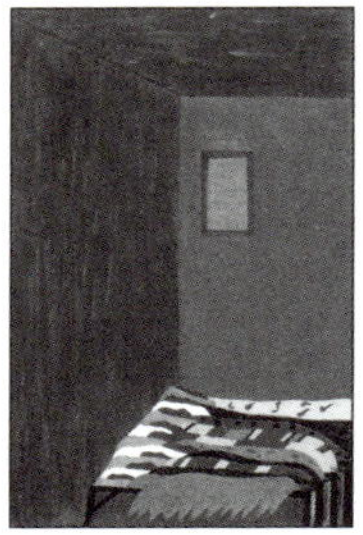

No. 47
As the migrant population grew, good housing became scarce. Workers were forced to live in overcrowded and dilapidated tenement houses.

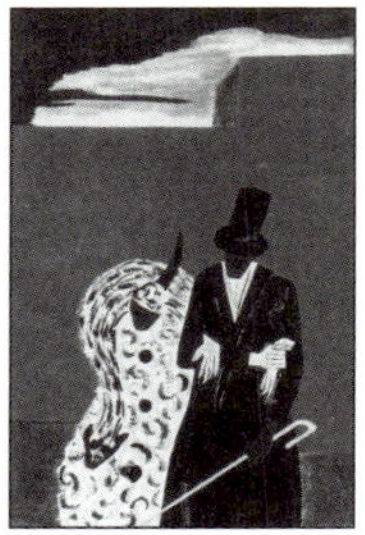

No. 53
African Americans who were long-time residents of northern cities met the migrants with aloofness and disdain.

Art Start

Draw a **narrative** series of pictures in the boxes below. Does your story have a **message** about something you would like to change? (If you don't like the size of these boxes or need more, create a new series on one of your "experiment pages.") For each drawing, write a **caption** that helps tell the story.

1

2

3

4

Experiment Page

Turn the page and a wish will be granted.

Your Wish Is *Granted!*

What if you had a great idea for a project. How would you pay for it? Artists, scientists, and writers apply for **grants** for all kinds of projects, from science to art.

Private foundations and branches of the government award thousands of grants each year for projects ranging from research on whales and water conservation to artmaking.

Art Start

Here is a grant application to get funding for an art project. Try filling it in. You can use your narrative art project. Use the space below to outline your ideas.

Project Title

It's always helpful to have a title for your project that is interesting and describes what your project is about.

Description

The project description is the most important part. You need to be very clear and direct. Focus your idea. Be bold!

Dates

How long will this project last? If you get the money, when do you plan to do the project? Will it take one week? two months? six months? a year?

Budget

This is where you say how much you think it will cost to make your project happen.

Budget Outline

This is where you list how much you think each item will cost. How much will you spend for supplies? To rent a studio? To rent or buy equipment? To pay your other bills while you are working on this project?

Schedule

Map out how long you think each stage of the project will take: research, writing, painting.

Grant Application

Name: ____________________

Address: ____________________

____

Title of project: ____________________

Project description: ____________________

____

____

____

____

Project dates: ____________________

Project budget: ____________________

Budget outline: ____________________

____

____

Project schedule: ____________________

____

____

____

____

Vocabulary

An art definition is given for each term definition. There might be another non-art definition for certain terms.

abstract when an artist does not show realistic objects, but uses lines, shapes, and colors to exaggerate or simplify something that he or she sees

asymmetrical balance when there is "visual balance" on either side of a composition's central line that is created by *different* kinds of lines, shapes, and colors

bodega a place where artists who work in different art forms share studio space

biomorphic shapes are based on nature, like animals or flowers, and often have more curved lines

depth illusion of 3-D space on a 2-D surface, like a picture of a ball on a piece of paper

gallery 1. a room in a museum; 2. a store where you can buy art

geometric shapes are based on geometry, like squares, rectangles, circles, triangles, and polygons

hue the artist's term for color

illusion something that isn't real, doesn't exist

light source provides an object or a scene with light; for example, the sun, or a lamp

line a point that moves through space and time

mentor a person who guides another person (usually younger) with advice, encouragement, and knowledge

mood the feeling created by a painting through color, line, and shape

museum a place where collected objects are stored and displayed

pattern when something is repeated like a line, shape, or color

picture plane the imaginary window surface of the paper or canvas used to talk about depth; when something is very close to the picture plane it looks very close

primary colors red, yellow, and blue; can be used to create all other colors

radial balance a composition that is the same from all sides

rhythm the even or uneven repetition of a visual, written, or musical pattern

secondary colors orange, purple, and green; made by mixing the primary colors

shape when two ends of a line meet they make a shape

space 1. the area of the paper or canvas you have on which to create; 2. the illusion of 3-D created by visual devices

symmetrical balance a composition where both sides are the same

value shades of light and dark

volume illusion of a 3-D object on a flat surface

Can You Find the Art Vocabulary Words in This Word Search?

R F G V M S D I A G O N A L E E C O L O R H F G N V X A N J P P M

A D E A A Y C C W E G H B A C Y P S N H V H V E R T I C A L R R G

D E F L R M P G O G R G N M A A E A N H J F A R G H F G H Y O I A

I Q S U I M O O Q M F U G B N G P N H Q D E R R D E V Q N B P M H

A W D E A E D A I B P A T C V B E T B S Q R I R G A O A S I O A S

L G H B N T G H B N A L R A G M K D I E D G E T G T L Y T O R R G

G B N S G R H J K S T J E J N K L P O O H F T C V E U A U M T Y N

P T N H T I F V C X T O B M R G D N B B N H Y A T R M A D O I F I

A V N A Y C T H L D G R F Q E U I D F J K S T H B S E B I R O J L

T H B P Q A H J B I H N A V Y N J S E C O N D A R Y W C O P N A E

T F B E K L E D X Z N R V C I A T C H O R I Z O N T A L X H S R E

E D M U S E U M G B N E D G T E G A B N M C N O I S U L L I C V F

R C B C H O I C E F B N S B H Q W C R H E N A L P E R U T C I P C

N U N I T Y F Q H Y A B R R O T N E M Y H B C P T N I T S P A C E

H U E G E O M E T R I C R M O O D F B D I R E C T I O N O I T O M

G H D I S T A N C E A N A R R A T I V E G B H D E P T H S H A D E

B A L A N C E F A S Y M M E T R I C A L E G E C R U O S T H G I L

F V A R T I S T S L A N G U A G E C R H Y T H M S H G A L L E R Y

Experiment Page

Experiment Page

Experiment Page

Experiment Page

Acknowledgments

It has been a pleasure to develop a handbook that combines two of my favorite topics: creating art and the creative process of Jacob Lawrence. I had the honor of meeting with Jacob Lawrence during children's programs in conjunction with the 1993 *Migration Series* exhibition. It goes without saying that this book is a form of dedication to him, his art, and his generous spirit. I would also like to thank Gwendolyn Knight Lawrence for her support of this project.

I would like to gratefully acknowledge my colleagues at The Phillips Collection, particularly Curator Elizabeth Hutton Turner for her guidance and profound understanding of Lawrence's art and life; Thora Colot and Ruth Perlin for their support; the staff of the Education Office, including Joanna Rothman, Shellie Marker, John McBrayer, and Vanessa Curtis for their creative ideas and feedback; and Maria Scarborough, our intern from the Maya Angelou Public Charter School for her invaluable "student's perspective."

I would also like to express my gratitude to Deba Leach for her collaboration and her thoughtful, thorough, and fun book on Lawrence; Gail Spilsbury for her considerate and much appreciated editing; and educators Judy Kramer and June Millikan for reading and responding to the manuscript.

I give deep thanks to my husband, Rustin Quaide, for his enthusiastic support.

The Phillips Collection is a magical place to bring children to experience the art of Jacob Lawrence. I owe a debt of gratitude to the Phillipses for their honest and fresh perspective on the world of art and the art of Jacob Lawrence.

Suzanne Wright
Director of Education
The Phillips Collection

All paintings by Jacob Lawrence except as noted. For all dimensions, height precedes width.

Front cover (also page 19)

Play Street, 1942. Gouache on paper, $30\frac{7}{8} \times 22\frac{3}{8}$ in. Collection Mrs. Stacey Clarfield Newman and Dr. Frederic Newman.

Photograph, Jacob Lawrence, age 6.

Photograph, Jacob Lawrence, 1939.

page 1 (also page 34)

Studio Corner, 1936. Watercolor on paper, $24\frac{1}{4} \times 18\frac{1}{4}$ in. Private collection.

page 2

Sidewalk Drawings, 1943. Gouache on paper, $22\frac{3}{8} \times 29\frac{1}{2}$ in. Collection J. Bruce Llewellyn and Shahara Ahmad-Llewellyn.

page 7

Self-Portrait, 1965. Brush and ink on paper, $15\frac{1}{4} \times 11\frac{5}{8}$ in. Courtesy Gwendolyn Knight Lawrence.

page 9 (also pages 23, 52)

From *The Migration of the Negro*, 1941. Casein tempera on hardboard, 12 × 18 in. The Phillips Collection, Washington, D.C. Panel 3: "In every town Negroes were leaving by the hundreds to go North and enter into Northern industry."

page 10 (also page 40)

From *The Migration of the Negro*, 1941. Casein tempera on hardboard, 12 × 18 in. The Phillips Collection, Washington, D.C. Panel 1: "During the World War there was a great migration North by Southern Negroes."

page 12

From *The Migration of the Negro*, 1941. Casein tempera on hardboard, 12 × 18 in. The Phillips Collection, Washington, D.C. Panel 31: "After arriving North the Negroes had better housing conditions."

page 14 (also pages 33, 52)

From *The Migration of the Negro*, 1941. Casein tempera on hardboard, 18 × 12 in. The Phillips Collection, Washington, D.C. Panel 47: "As well as finding better housing conditions in the North, the migrants found very poor housing conditions in the North. They were forced into overcrowded and dilapidated tenement houses."

page 16

The Homecoming, 1936. Tempera on brown paper, 35 × 22 in. Collection Mrs. Daniel Cowin.

page 19

Play Street. See front cover.

page 20

Peddlers Reduce Their Prices in the Evening to Get Rid of Their Perishables, 1943. Gouache on paper, $15\frac{1}{8} \times 22\frac{5}{8}$ in. Countee Cullen Art Collection, Hampton University Museum, Hampton, Virginia.

page 23 top

Detail, *The Migration of the Negro*, Panel 3. See page 9.

page 23 bottom (also page 29)

Chow, 1936. Graphite on paper, 9 × 6 in. Spelman College, Atlanta.

page 24

Jacob Lawrence (second from left) making block prints in the Harlem art workshop, c. 1933–34. Charles Alston, 1930s.

page 26 (also page 52)

From *The Migration of the Negro*, 1941. Casein tempera on hardboard, 12 × 18 in. The Phillips Collection, Washington, D.C. Panel 45: "They arrived in Pittsburgh, one of the great industrial centers of the North, in large numbers."

page 29

Chow. See page 23.

page 31

Artists of "306" Studio, late 1930s. National Archives, Harmon Foundation Collection.

page 32

Ironers, 1943. Gouache on paper, $21\frac{3}{8} \times 29\frac{1}{2}$ in. Private Collection.

page 33

The Migration of the Negro, Panel 47. See page 14.

page 34

Studio Corner. See page 1.

page 36 top

Bartolomeo di Tommaso, *The Lamentation and the Entombment*. The Metropolitan Museum of Art, Gwynne Andrews Fund, 1958. (58.87.2) Photograph © 1988 The Metropolitan Museum of Art.

page 36 bottom

Goblet in the form of a human head, Zaïre. Musée de l'Homme, Paris. Photograph © Musée de l'Homme.

page 38

The Life of Toussaint L'Ouverture, No. 20, 1938. Tempera on paper, $19 \times 11\frac{1}{2}$ in. Amistad Research Center, Tulane University, New Orleans, Aaron Douglas Collection.

page 40

The Migration of the Negro, Panel 1. See page 10.

page 44

Vaudeville, 1951. Egg tempera on hardboard with pencil, $29\frac{7}{8} \times 20$ in. Hirshhorn Museum and Sculpture Garden, Smithsonian Institution. Gift of Joseph H. Hirshhorn, 1966.

page 52

From *The Migration of the Negro*, 1941. Casein tempera on hardboard, 12 × 18 in. or 18 × 12 in. The Phillips Collection, Washington, D.C. Panel 3: see page 9. Panel 45: see page 26. Panel 47: see page 14. Panel 53: "African Americans, long-time residents of northern cities, met the migrants with aloofness and disdain."

Published by
The Phillips Collection
1600 Twenty-first Street, NW
Washington, D.C. 20009-1090
www.phillipscollection.org

ISBN: 0-943044-30-8

Editor: Gail Spilsbury
Design concept: Suzanne Wright
Designed by John Hubbard
Illustrations by Amy Cilléy
Color separations by iocolor, Seattle
Produced by Marquand Books, Inc., Seattle
www.marquand.com
Printed and bound by CS Graphics Pte., Ltd., Singapore